Tishray

Rosh Hashana
Yom Kippur
Sukkos
Shmini Atzeres
Simchas Torah

Teves

Assara B'Teves

Cheshvan

Shvat

Shabbas Shira
Tu B'Shvat
Parashas Shekalim

Kislev

Chanuka

Adar

Parashas Zachor
Taanis Ester
Purim
Parashas Parah
Parashas Hachodesh

FOLLOW THE MOON

A JOURNEY THROUGH THE JEWISH YEAR

written by Yaffa Ganz

design and illustrations by Harvey Klineman

FELDHEIM PUBLISHERS · JERUSALEM · NEW YORK

Except for place names in Israel, the Ashkenazic pronunciation of the Hebrew is used throughout *Follow the Moon*. All Hebrew and Yiddish words, except for well known holidays, are explained in the text or in the glossary at the end of the book. ▪ There are differing opinions regarding the dates of certain events in Jewish history. For purposes of simplicity, the most widely accepted dates are usually the ones given. ▪ The author wishes to acknowledge her debt of gratitude to Eliyahu Kitov, z''l, from whose encyclopedic work *Sefer Hatodaah* (The Book of Our Heritage) much of the information in this book was culled.

First published 1984
ISBN 0-87306-369-4

Philipp Feldheim Inc.
200 Airport Executive Park
Spring Valley, NY 10977

Printed in Israel

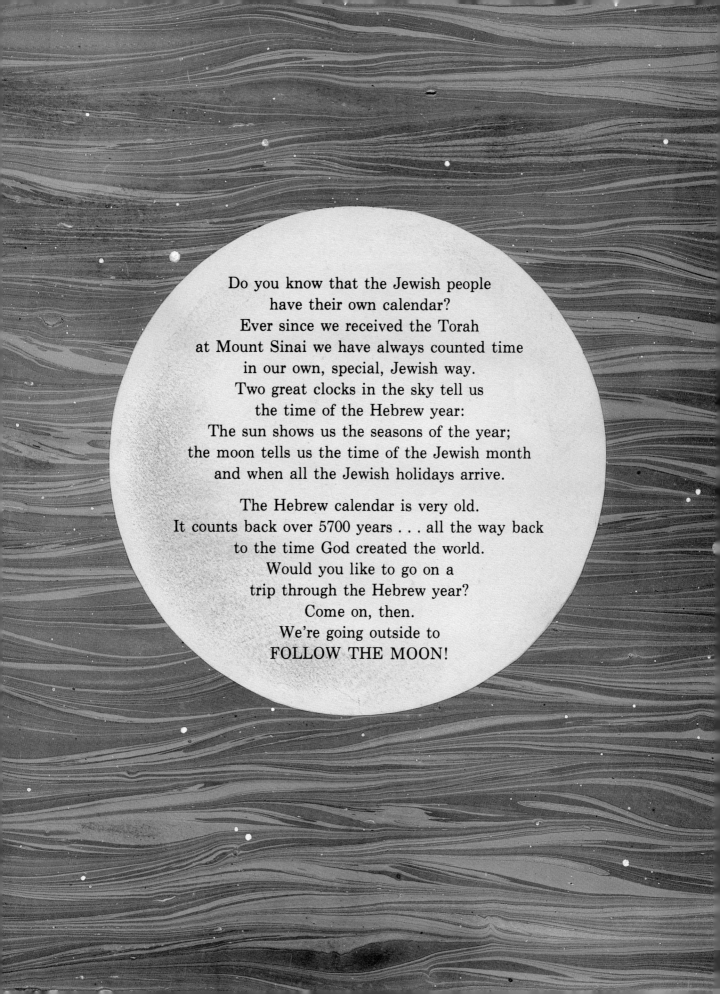

Do you know that the Jewish people
have their own calendar?
Ever since we received the Torah
at Mount Sinai we have always counted time
in our own, special, Jewish way.
Two great clocks in the sky tell us
the time of the Hebrew year:
The sun shows us the seasons of the year;
the moon tells us the time of the Jewish month
and when all the Jewish holidays arrive.

The Hebrew calendar is very old.
It counts back over 5700 years . . . all the way back
to the time God created the world.
Would you like to go on a
trip through the Hebrew year?
Come on, then.
We're going outside to
FOLLOW THE MOON!

Look . . . up in the sky. Do you see the moon?
It's a *Rosh Chodesh* moon—a brand-new skinny silvery slice of moon.
A *Rosh Chodesh* moon means we're at the beginning of a new Hebrew month.
Every month, the moon moves in a big ring around the earth.
It gets bigger and bigger, until it is a full circle of light in the sky.
Then it gets smaller and smaller, until it finally disappears.
That's when the Hebrew month is over, and it's time for a new month to begin.

Long ago in *Eretz Yisrael*, in the days of the *Sanhedrin*, at the end
of each month the rabbis would wait for two people to come and say,
"We've seen the new moon!"
Then the *Sanhedrin* would sanctify the month, bless it, and announce that
a new Hebrew month had begun. Do you know how they told everyone?
They lit five huge fires on the tops of five high mountains so that
everyone in and around *Eretz Yisrael* would see the flames.
Nowadays we have no *Sanhedrin*, but we do have the calendar

Rosh Chodesh
רֹאשׁ חוֹדֶשׁ

which the rabbis of the *Talmud* calculated and handed down to us.
We can look at it and see exactly when *Rosh Chodesh* will arrive.
Someday, when the *beis hamikdash* is rebuilt and the *Sanhedrin* meets
in Jerusalem again, perhaps *you* will be one of the witnesses to see the new moon!
There are twelve months in a Hebrew year, except in a leap year
when there are thirteen.
Each month is either twenty-nine or thirty days long.
Every year, twelve groups of stars move across the sky.
They are the twelve *mazalos*—the constellations. Each month has its own *mazal*.

In Hebrew,
the moon has two names—
YAREYACH and LEVANA.
The word "month"
has two names too—
CHODESH from the word
chadash (new) and
YERACH from the word
yareyach (moon).

On the *Shabbos* before each *Rosh Chodesh*,
we welcome the new month with *birkas hachodesh*.
We ask *Hashem* to bless the month and to fill it
with health and long life and peace for all Jews
everywhere. And we ask Him to please hurry
and bring all of the Jewish people back
to the Land of Israel.

One night each month
we go outside to say
kiddush levana—
a blessing on the moon.

Rosh Chodesh is a special holiday gift to the
women of Israel because they did not take part
in the sin of the Golden Calf. On *Rosh Chodesh*,
Jewish women do not do any unnecessary work.

Did you know that the rabbis compared the Jewish people to the moon?
Just like the moon, we are sometimes small and weak and our light seems dim.
But like the moon, we will always grow bigger and brighter and stronger again.

Nissan
נִיסָן

The Hebrew year has more
than one beginning.
Rosh Hashana, the Head of the Year,
comes in the month of *Tishray*.
But we count the Hebrew months
from the month of NISSAN, because NISSAN is a beginning too.
The Torah tells us: "This month shall be the beginning of your months.
It shall be the first month of your year."

NISSAN comes in the spring when a new year begins
for all the things that grow. How busy everything is in NISSAN!
The earth wakes up after the cold winter. The animals give birth
to their young; and the trees and plants start to bud and flower,
painting the world in a rainbow of colors.

And how busy *we* are in NISSAN—
carefully cleaning the house and removing
all the *chametz* and preparing for *Pesach*.
For great miracles happened in the month of NISSAN.
On the eve of the 15th of NISSAN,
the Jews made ready to leave
the Land of Egypt.

They hurriedly ate the *matza* and *maror* together with the lambs they had slaughtered for the *korban pesach*, just as *Hashem* had commanded.

Pesach means *passed over*, for the Angel of Death was given a sign. He *passed over* all the Jewish homes where blood from the *korban pesach* had been smeared on the doorposts.

Meanwhile, God sent the tenth and last plague to punish the Egyptians. The Angel of Death was commanded to kill all of Egypt's firstborn. Only the Jews were spared.

Early the next morning, God freed His people from their slavery, and with a mighty hand and an outstretched arm, He took them out of the land of Egypt. They left in such haste that there was no time for their dough to rise or for them to bake their bread.

Therefore, on the eve of the 15th of NISSAN, we sit down to the first *seder* to celebrate and remember *yetzias Mitzrayim*. We eat *matza* and *maror* and drink four cups of wine, and we read the *haggada* from beginning to end. In Israel there is one *seder* and seven days of *Pesach*; in *chutz la'aretz* there are two *sedarim* and eight days.

NISSAN is called *Hachodesh Harishon* — the First Month — because we count our months from the time *Hashem* took us out of Egypt.

The *Shabbos* before *Pesach* is called *Shabbos Hagadol* — the Great Sabbath.

During NISSAN the roads in *Eretz Yisrael* were very full. *Pesach* is the first of the *shalosh regalim*, the three great pilgrimages when all of *bnei Yisrael* went up to Jerusalem and the *beis hamikdash*.

After wandering in the desert for forty years, the Jewish people crossed the Jordan River and entered the Land of Israel on the tenth of NISSAN.

NISSAN is thirty days long and it has three different names —
HACHODESH HARISHON: the first month
CHODESH HA'AVIV: the month of spring, and
NISSAN, of course!

Moshe Rabbaynu's sister Miriam died on the tenth of NISSAN. *Hashem* had given the Jewish people a wonderful gift in honor of Miriam — a well of clear, cool water which followed them all through the desert. When Miriam died, the well dried up and disappeared.

Once every twenty-eight years in the month of NISSAN we say *birkas hachama*, a blessing on the sun. The last time was in the Hebrew year 5741. Figure out for yourself when the next time will be!

The *mazal* for NISSAN is a lamb. It reminds us of the lamb used for the *korban pesach*.

Iyar
אִיָּר

IYAR is the second month in the Jewish year. It is also called *Ziv*, the Month of Brightness, because during each of its twenty-nine days the sun rises higher in the spring sky, making the world lighter and warmer.

The *mazal* for IYAR is an ox.

Shlomo Hamelech began to build the first *beis hamikdash* on the first of IYAR. On the same day, four hundred and eighty years later, *Ezra Hasofer* started building the second *beis hamikdash*.

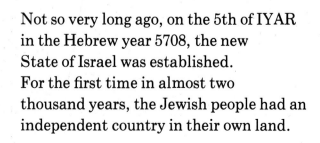

Not so very long ago, on the 5th of IYAR in the Hebrew year 5708, the new State of Israel was established. For the first time in almost two thousand years, the Jewish people had an independent country in their own land.

The 14th of IYAR is *Pesach Shayni*— the Second Pesach. Anyone who could not bring the *Pesach* sacrifice to Jerusalem in *Nissan* could bring it on *Pesach Shayni*, one month later.

Lag Ba'omer, the 33rd day of the Counting of the Omer, is on the 18th of IYAR. *Lag Ba'omer* is a day of weddings, and of picnics and bows and arrows in memory of Rabbi Akiva and his students. And a *Yom Hilula* for Shimon bar Yochai. Bonfires are lit all over Israel, especially at his grave in Meron, and little boys come there for their first haircut.

The 28th of IYAR in the year 5727 was a day of great victory, thanksgiving and rejoicing for the Jewish people. On that day, in the midst of a fierce six-day war, Jerusalem was reunited. The Old City and the *Kotel Hama'aravi* were returned to *Am Yisrael*. Ask your parents and grandparents to tell you all about it!

Sivan
סִיוָן

SIVAN is the third month in our calendar. The most important thing that ever happened to the Jewish people happened in the month of SIVAN.

On the 6th day of SIVAN, 2448 years after the creation of the world, the Jewish people received the Torah at *Har Sinai*.

There are thirty days in SIVAN, and the *mazal* for the month is twins.

The 6th of SIVAN is called *Z'man Matan Torasaynu* — the Time of the Giving of Our Torah — but it has four more names as well. Do you think you can remember them all?

* CHAG HASHAVUOS: the Festival of Weeks. We count forty-nine days — seven weeks — from *Pesach* until *Shavuos*.
* CHAG HAKATZIR: the holiday of the spring harvest
* CHAG HABIKURIM: the holiday of the first fruit offering
* ATZERES: a day of assembly

Shavuos is the second of the *shalosh regalim*. Jews from all over *Eretz Yisrael* came up to Jerusalem in a great, winding procession, bringing the first ripened fruits from their fields to the *beis hamikdash*.

On *Shavuos* we read the story of Ruth, the princess from the land of Moav who accepted the Torah and all of the *mitzvos* and came to live in *Eretz Yisrael*. Ruth was the great-grandmother of David, King of Israel.

David Hamelech was born on the 6th of SIVAN. Seventy years later, he died on the same date.

And did you know that on the 6th of SIVAN, Pharaoh's daughter Bithya pulled a basket of reeds out of the river? She found a baby boy inside whom she named *Moshe*!

Tammuz
תַּמּוּז

TAMMUZ is the fourth month in our year and the first month of the summer. The sun is high in the sky and you have twenty-nine long days to think about picnics and vacations and ice-cream cones!

Did you ever hear of the sun and moon standing still? Long long ago, on the 3rd of TAMMUZ, the Jews fought a fierce battle against the Amorites in the valley of Ayalon in the Land of Israel. When *Yehoshua* lifted his hands up high, God made the sun and the moon pause in the sky so the Jews could rout their enemies before the night began.

Moshe came down from Mt. Sinai on *Shiv'a Assar B'Tammuz* — the 17th of TAMMUZ. He was carrying the *luchos habris*, the two stone tablets with the Ten Commandments.

But when he saw the Jews dancing around a Golden Calf, he was so full of sorrow and anger that he threw the heavy tablets down. They fell to the ground and shattered into a zillion tiny pieces.

Shiv'a Assar B'Tammuz is a day of fasting. On this day, the enemies of the Jewish people broke through the thick walls surrounding Jerusalem and entered the city to destroy it. The three weeks between the 17th of *Tammuz* and the 9th of *Av* are a time of mourning for us. There are no weddings or parties or other celebrations during these three weeks. We don't listen to music either.

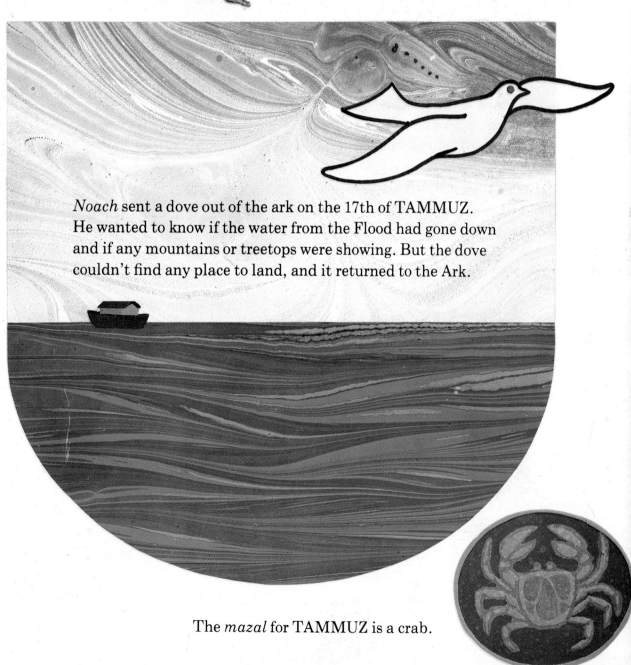

Noach sent a dove out of the ark on the 17th of TAMMUZ. He wanted to know if the water from the Flood had gone down and if any mountains or treetops were showing. But the dove couldn't find any place to land, and it returned to the Ark.

The *mazal* for TAMMUZ is a crab.

AV is the fifth month in the Hebrew year. It is a month of sorrow and mourning, for both *batei mikdash* were destroyed in AV.

But it is also called *Menachem Av*, because someday, *Hashem* will comfort the Jewish people in this month. The *beis hamikdash* will be rebuilt, and AV will become a month of joy. There are 30 days in AV, and the *mazal* is a lion.

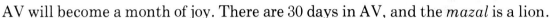

Aaron, the brother of *Moshe*, died on the first of AV, 40 years after the Jews left Egypt.

The twelve *meraglim* who were sent to explore the Land of Israel returned on the 9th of AV. But instead of praising the rich, fruitful land *Hashem* had promised them, ten of the *meraglim* — all except *Yehoshua* and *Kalev* — complained. When the rest of the people complained along with them, *Hashem* was very angry. Instead of bringing them right into *Eretz Yisrael*, He made them wander in the desert for forty years.

The first *beis hamikdash* was destroyed on *Tisha B'Av*, the 9th day in AV. Over five hundred years later, the second *beis hamikdash* was destroyed on the very same date. *Tisha B'Av* is a day of fasting and prayer.

In the same year that Columbus was busy discovering America, a terrible calamity befell the Jews of Spain. King Ferdinand and Queen Isabella decreed that all the Jews must leave the country. On a bitter *Tisha B'Av* morning, 300,000 Jewish men, women and children were driven out of Spain with nothing more than the food they could carry. They began a long, frightful journey, with no place to go.

But *Tisha B'Av* is also a time of hope. *Mashiach* was born on *Tisha B'Av*. When it's time for him to come, all the Jews will return to the Land of Israel and the third *beis hamikdash* will be built.

After forty years in the desert, on the 15th of AV, God forgave the Jews for the sin of the *meraglim*. That's why *Tu B'Av* became a festival of joy and forgiveness. On that day, the daughters of Israel dressed in white clothing and went out to dance in the vineyards in *Eretz Yisrael*. It became the perfect day for Jewish weddings. In fact, it still is!

Elul
אֱלוּל

ELUL is the 6th month in the year. It comes at the end of the summer, one month before *Rosh Hashana*. It is a special month for doing *teshuva*. Each weekday morning in ELUL we blow the *shofar* to remind us that *Rosh Hashana* and *Yom Kippur* will be here soon.

ELUL has twenty-nine days, and its *mazal* is a young maiden.

ANI L'DODI V'DODI LI — I BELONG TO MY BELOVED AND MY BELOVED BELONGS TO ME

אֲנִי לְדוֹדִי וְדוֹדִי לִי

In Hebrew, the initials of the words *Ani L'dodi V'dodi Li* spell the word ELUL. *Hashem* is the "Beloved" of the Jewish people.

Remember the ten spies? They died on the 17th of ELUL, forty days after they complained about the Land of Israel.

The week before *Rosh Hashana*, either late at night or very early in the morning, we go to the synagogue to say *selichos*.

ELUL is a good time to bring your *mezuzos* and *tefillin* to a *sofer*. He will check the insides to make sure they are in perfect condition. If any of the letters are smeared or cracked or erased, he will fix them.

Tishray
תִּשְׁרֵי

The *mazal* for TISHRAY is a pair of scales because this is the month when God "weighs" our deeds and judges the world.

We count our months from *Nissan* when the Jews left Egypt, but our years begin with TISHRAY when God created the world. So even though TISHRAY is the seventh month, it is the beginning of the new Hebrew year.

TISHRAY is *Yerach Ha'eysanim* — the Month of the Mighty Ones — because *Avraham*, *Yitzchak* and *Yaakov* were born in TISHRAY. It is a busy month with thirty important, joyous days and many, many *mitzvos*. TISHRAY is a time for *teshuva*, *tefilla* and *tzedaka*, and for listening to the sound of the *shofar*. It's a time for apples and honey and round *challos*, for waving the *lulav* and *esrog*, and for sitting in the *sukka* with lots of friends. It's a time for being happy and thankful for belonging to *Am Yisrael*!

The first and second days of TISHRAY are *Rosh Hashana*, the beginning of our year.

Rosh Hashana is also called

YOM HAZIKARON: the Day of Remembrance
YOM HADIN: the Day of Judgment
YOM HAKESEH: the Day of Concealment

On *Rosh Hashana* God REMEMBERS everything we've done all year long. He JUDGES all of our deeds and decides what our new year will be like. Will we be rich or poor? Healthy or sick? Will there be peace or war? And will we be blessed with the gift of life? Everything is hidden and CONCEALED from us. We don't know what *Hashem* will decide. Even the moon is "concealed." *Rosh Hashana* is the only holiday which falls on the first of the month when the new moon may not yet be visible in the sky. We pray that God will decree a year of life and blessing for us as we fill the month with

TESHUVA . . . TEFILLA . . . TZEDAKA
mending our ways, prayers, and charity!

How do you greet your
friends on *Rosh Hashana*?

כְּתִיבָה וַחֲתִימָה טוֹבָה

With a KESIVA VACHASIMA TOVA —
May You Be Inscribed
in the Book of Life!

The first ten days of TISHRAY, from *Rosh Hashana* to *Yom Kippur*, are the
Asseres Y'may Teshuva—the Ten Days of Repentance. The 3rd of TISHRAY is
Tzom Gedalya—the Fast of *Gedalya*.

Yom Kippur is the 10th day of the month. It has always been a day of forgiveness
for the Jewish people. On *Yom Kippur*, God forgave the Jews for having made
the Golden Calf. He sent *Moshe Rabbaynu* down from *Har Sinai* with two new
luchos habris. This time, *Moshe* didn't break them.

When the long day of fasting
and prayer is over, we go outside
to say the blessing on the new moon.
We wish each other a good year
and go home to eat a joyful meal.
Then we get to work on
building our *sukka*!

Sukkos begins on the 15th of TISHRAY.
In Israel, *Sukkos* is seven days long.
In *chutz la'aretz*, it is eight.

The *sukka* reminds us of the forty
years the Jews wandered in the desert
with no real homes.
It reminds us of their trust
and faith in *Hashem*.
It reminds us of the Clouds of Glory
which protected them from the hot
sun and the cold nights.
And it reminds us of *Eretz Yisrael*,
because *Sukkos* is *Chag Ha'asif*—
a time of thanksgiving when
the summer crops are gathered in
from the fields in Israel.

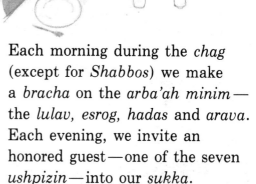

Each morning during the *chag*
(except for *Shabbos*) we make
a *bracha* on the *arba'ah minim*—
the *lulav, esrog, hadas* and *arava*.
Each evening, we invite an
honored guest—one of the seven
ushpizin—into our *sukka*.

Sukkos was the third great yearly pilgrimage to
Jerusalem. Everyone wanted to perform the
mitzva of *aliya la'regel* and no one wanted to miss
the *Sukkos* celebrations in the *beis hamikdash*.
Especially the *Simchas Beis Hasho'ayva*—
the Celebration in Honor of the Drawing of the Water.

After *Hoshana Rabba* (the last day
of *Sukkos*) comes *Shmini Atzeres*,
an *extra* day of rejoicing. That's
when we pray for the rains to fall in
Eretz Yisrael.

And then it's time for *Simchas Torah*!
We finish reading the Torah
and begin at the beginning again.
But not before we go seven times
round, dancing and singing with the
sifray Torah. Seven *hakafos* at night
and seven *hakafos* next morning.

Cheshvan
חֶשְׁוָן

CHESHVAN, the 8th month of the year, has arrived.
It is a quiet month after all the excitement of *Tishray*.
The weather is getting colder, and the wind is
starting to blow the leaves off the trees.
In Israel, the blue summer skies are turning cloudy
and gray as the rainy season approaches.

CHESHVAN is called *Marcheshvan*—a bitter month. Do you know why it has such a
strange name? Because there are no holidays in this month. Of course *that* means we
can have an entire, uninterrupted month to learn Torah!

On the 7th of CHESHVAN, Jews in *Eretz Yisrael* begin to say the prayer
V'sayn tal u'matar livracha—May You give the dew and rain for a blessing.

The Great Flood began on the 17th of CHESHVAN. For forty days and forty nights the rain poured down in torrents while *Noach* and his family floated safely in the Ark. Perhaps that is why CHESHVAN is also called *Bul*—from the Hebrew word *mabul*—flood.

Noach came out of the Ark on the 28th of CHESHVAN, one year and eleven days after the Flood began. He built an altar and offered a sacrifice to thank *Hashem* for having saved him and his family.

Shlomo Hamelech finished building the first *beis hamikdash* in the month of CHESHVAN.

Rachel Imaynu died on the 11th of CHESHVAN. She was buried in *Beit Lechem*, not far from Jerusalem. Ever since then, and especially on the 11th of CHESHVAN, Jews have gone to *Kever Rachel* to pray. If you are in *Eretz Yisrael*, you can go too.

CHESHVAN has either 29 or 30 days, and the *mazal* for the month is a scorpion.

Kislev כִּסְלֵו

KISLEV is the ninth month in our year.
It is either 29 or 30 days long.
KISLEV is cold outdoors, but inside, our houses are full
of the light and the warmth of the *Chanuka* candles.

The *mazal* for KISLEV is a bow, to remind us of the rainbow.

God blessed *Noach* in the beginning of KISLEV and showed him
the world's first rainbow. It was a sign and a promise that the world
would never be destroyed by a flood again.

On the 25th of KISLEV, the Jews
finished building the *mishkan* in the desert.
And on the 25th of KISLEV, almost
one thousand years later,
they celebrated the beginning of
the rebuilding of the second
beis hamikdash. But the most famous
25th of KISLEV was in the Hebrew
year 3597 when the Jewish nation
celebrated the first *Chanuka*!

That day, the Jews won a great
victory over their enemies.
Mattisyahu and his five sons
led the tiny Jewish army against
the great Hellenist-Syrian king
Antiochus. They drove him and his
vast armies out of Jerusalem
and *Eretz Yisrael*.

The *Chashmona'im* removed the idols and purified the *beis hamikdash*, rededicating it to *Hashem*. But when they wanted to light the *menora*, there was only enough pure olive oil to last for one day. That's when the *nes* — the miracle — of *Chanuka* took place. *Hashem* made the oil last for eight whole days until new oil could be prepared.

Since then, *Chanuka* is eight days of *Hallel* and *dreidles* and *latkes* and *Chanuka gelt*, of light and thanksgiving and joy and hope for all Jews everywhere. We hope we will be able to dedicate a new *beis hamikdash* soon. And who knows . . . perhaps it will even be on the 25th of KISLEV!

The word *Chanuka* has two meanings:
    CHANUKA = dedication (of the *beis hamikdash*)
    CHANU = they rested; KA = (on) the 25th (of KISLEV)

Did you know
— that when the Jews were wandering in the desert, the 25th place they camped at was called CHASHMONA?
— that the 25th word in the Torah is OR (light)?

Teves

טֵבֵת

TEVES, the tenth month in the year, is twenty-nine days long. In Israel, the cold winter rains are still falling, filling the empty riverbeds and wells and lakes, and seeping deep down into the ground.

Sometimes, in the mountains of Jerusalem or *Tzfat* or the *Chermon*, it even snows.

TEVES begins on the sixth or the seventh day of *Chanuka*. So even though there are no other holidays this month, we still have a little bit of *Chanuka* left to enjoy.

On the 8th of TEVES, King Ptolemy of Egypt forced seventy-two Jewish sages to translate the Torah into the Greek language. Ptolemy made each of the sages sit alone in a different place and translate the entire Torah by himself. He was sure that each sage would write something different. But God caused a miracle to happen.

All seventy-two sages translated the Torah in exactly the same way.

Assara B'Teves, the 10th of TEVES,
is a day of fasting. On this day,
in the time of the First Temple,
Nevuchadnetzar, king of Babylon,
began to attack the city of Jerusalem.
For two long years he laid seige
to the city until finally, in the third year,
he broke through the heavy walls
and entered *Yerushalayim*.

Two great and beloved leaders —
Ezra Hasofer and *Nechemya* —
brought the Jews back from Babylon
to *Eretz Yisrael* to build the Second Temple.
The date of their death —
the 9th of TEVES — was a day
of deep sorrow and mourning.

The *mazal* for the month of TEVES is a goat.

Shvat

שְׁבָט

SHVAT is the eleventh month in the year. It has thirty days.

The *mazal* for SHVAT is a vessel filled with water.

On the first of SHVAT, in the fortieth year in the desert, *Moshe Rabbaynu* began to review all of the Torah with the Jewish people. He went over all the laws, taught the people new *mitzvos*, and blessed them. For thirty-seven days he spoke to them and taught them. These were the last thirty-seven days of his life.

When did *Moshe* and the Jewish people sing?
On the 7th day of *Pesach*, when God split the *Yam Suf* and let the people pass safely through. That's when they sang *Shiras Hayam* — a song of praise at the sea.
We read *Shiras Hayam* in the Torah on *Shabbas Shira* in the month of SHVAT.
Some people leave crumbs out for the birds on *Shabbas Shira* because the birds sing God's praises *every* day of the year.

By *Tu B'Shvat*, the 15th of SHVAT,
the long winter is coming to an end.
Tiny bumpy buds are pushing their way out
of all the branches, and the almond trees are
already in bloom. They look just like wispy round
bunches of soft, white cotton candy!

Tu B'Shvat is *Rosh Hashana La'ilanos*,
a New Year for the Trees. On *Tu B'Shvat*,
God renews the strength and fertility
of *Eretz Yisrael*, and when the Land of Israel
is rich and fertile, the People of Israel
give thanks and are happy.
We celebrate *Tu B'Shvat* by eating
fruits grown in *Eretz Yisrael*. And if
you're lucky enough to be there
you can plant a tree — in honor of
Rosh Hashana La'ilanos and in order to
make *Eretz Yisrael* a more beautiful,
fruitful country!

Every Jew was commanded to give one half-*shekel*
for the sacrifices in the *beis hamikdash* each year.
We read about it in the Torah on *Parashas Shekalim*,
the last *Shabbos* in SHVAT.

Adar
אֲדָר

מִשֶּׁנִּכְנַס אֲדָר מַרְבִּים בְּשִׂמְחָה

When ADAR begins, our joy increases!

The *mazal* for ADAR is fish, a symbol of good fortune and blessings.

Hold on to your hats! Here come twenty-nine days of joy for the Jewish people! Can you guess why? Because *Purim* comes in ADAR!

On the *Shabbos* before *Purim, Parashas Zachor*, we read about God's command to destroy the evil Amalek and all of his descendants. Haman was a descendant of Amalek.

Queen Esther fasted and prayed for three days before she asked King Achashverosh if he would help save the Jews. We fast only one day — on *Taanis Ester*, the 13th of ADAR. The 14th of ADAR is *Purim*, a day of victory and rejoicing. You'll hear the whole story — all about Mordechai, Esther, King Achashverosh, Queen Vashti, and of course, Haman — when we read the *megilla* on *Purim*. In fact, you'll hear it twice — once in the evening and once in the morning. Don't forget to bring your *groggers*!

In the walled city of Shushan, the Jews celebrated *Purim* on the 15th of ADAR instead of the 14th. That's why, in *Yerushalayim* and the other walled cities of *Eretz Yisrael*, *Purim* is celebrated on the 15th of ADAR.

Moshe Rabbaynu was born on the 7th of ADAR. On the 7th of ADAR, one hundred and twenty years later, he died.

On the 15th of ADAR, after the winter rains were over, workmen were sent out to fix the roads in *Eretz Yisrael*. It's easy to guess why. Because tens of thousands of *olei regel* would soon be coming up to Jerusalem and the *beis hamikdash* for *Pesach*!

The third or fourth *Shabbos* in ADAR (depending on the year) is *Parashas Parah*, when we read about the *parah adumah*—the laws dealing with the Red Heifer.

Do you remember that in a Hebrew leap year there are thirteen months instead of twelve? The thirteenth month is called ADAR SHAYNI—the second ADAR. There is an ADAR SHAYNI in our calendar seven times every nineteen years.

On *Parashas Hachodesh* we announce the coming of the month of *Nissan*. We read in the Torah: "This month [*Nissan*] shall be the beginning of your months. It shall be the first month of your year." *Parashas Hachodesh* tells us that we have finished another cycle in the Jewish year. The moon has circled around the earth twelve more times and has brought us twelve more months of miracles, *mitzvos* and *chagim*; of Torah, blessings, hope and joy. Twelve months of Jewish time—made holy by the Jewish people.

Would you like to begin again? It's easy! Just go outside, look up at the sky, and . . .
FOLLOW THE MOON!

Although we've gone through the entire Hebrew year,
there is still one VERY IMPORTANT DATE which is
missing. It isn't printed on any Jewish calendar,
but it's a date you should know and remember.

Here is an entire page for you to record it
in big, clear letters . . .

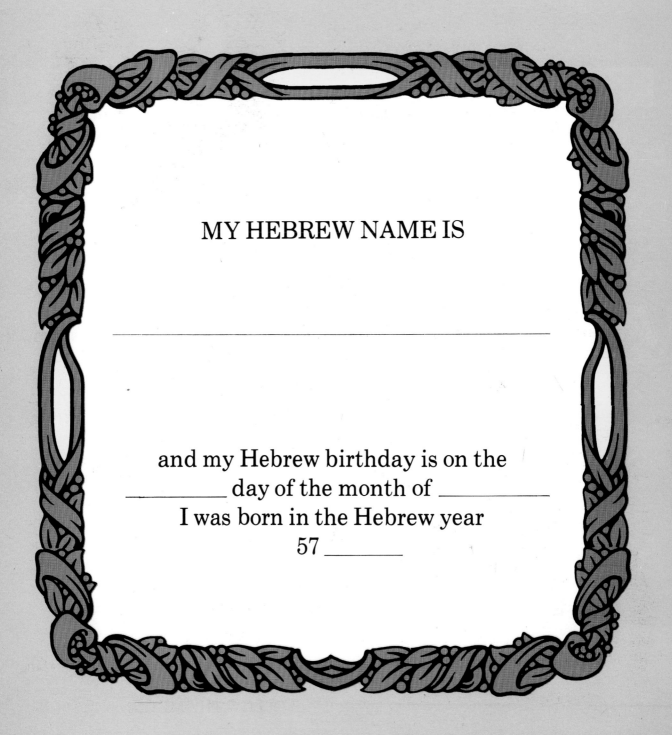

MY HEBREW NAME IS

_____

and my Hebrew birthday is on the
_____ day of the month of _____
I was born in the Hebrew year
57 _____

glossary of Hebrew

aliya la'regel: pilgrimage to the Temple in Jerusalem

Am Yisrael: the People of Israel

arava: willow

arba'ah minim: the four plants used for a blessing during Sukkos

Avraham: the patriarch Abraham

batei mikdash: plural of *beis hamikdash*

beis hamikdash: the Holy Temple in Jerusalem

Beit Lechem: Bethlehem

birkas hachodesh: the blessing for the new month

bnei Yisrael: the Jewish people

bracha: a blessing

chag (chagim): holiday

Chag Ha'asif: harvest-time

challos: special white bread for the Sabbath and the holidays

chametz: leavened foods, forbidden on Pesach

Chanuka gelt: gifts of money for Chanuka

Chashmona'im: the Hasmonean family

Chermon: Mount Hermon

chutz la'aretz: any place outside the Land of Israel

David Hamelech: King David

dreidles: spinning tops (Yiddish)

Eretz Yisrael: the Land of Israel

esrog: citron

Ezra Hasofer: Ezra the Scribe

groggers: noisemakers for Purim (Yiddish)

hadas: myrtle

haggada: the story of the Redemption from Egypt, read at the seder

hakafos: marching with the Torah scrolls

Hallel: a prayer of praise to God

Har Sinai: Mount Sinai

Hashem: God

Kalev: Caleb, one of the leaders of the tribe of Judah

Kever Rachel: Rachel's Tomb

korban pesach: the Passover sacrifice

Kotel Hama'aravi: the Western Wall

latkes: potato pancakes (Yiddish)

luchos habris: Tablets of the Covenant (the Ten Commandments)

lulav: palm branch

maror: bitter herbs

Mashiach: the Messiah

Mattisyahu: Mattathias the High Priest

matza: unleavened bread

mazal (mazalos): constellation

megilla: scroll